God Sent The Raven

RAVEN CHASITY ROGERS

Table of Contents

Dedication   ix
Foreword   xi
Tremayne Moore, Author & Publisher

PART 1: IT IS GOD!

God Sent The Raven!!!	3
Dear Blue Skies	4
Stargaze	5
The Author of My Soul	6
The Essence of You	7
That Sunday Flow	9
The Ultimate Homie	10
Reflection	11

PART 2: IT IS ME!

A Mirror of Me	15
Glisten Me, Please!	16
I'm a Better Woman! For a Better Man!	17
Thankfully Single	18
The Power of My Tears	19
You Can't Put Out My Fire	20
Reflection	21

PART 3: IT IS LOVE!

2 Different Time Zones of Love	25
A Bittersweet Lullaby	26
A Lovely Valentine	27
Crimson Love	28
My Perky Love!	29

Rose Petals	30
Our Absolute Love	31
The Compass to My Heart	32
Reflection	33

PART 4: IT IS GREAT!

A Glimpse of Fresh Air	37
That Great Commencement!	38
The Runway of Victory!!!	40
Reflection	41

PART 5: IT IS FAMILY!

Four: Four: Four (444)	45
I Cried for You	46
My Daddy! My Heart!	47
Sixteen Crystals	48
Reflection	49

PART 6: IT IS CLEAR!

A Tailored Lie	53
Distant Waves	54
If I Have to Beg	55
Invisible Butterfly	56
The Looking Glass	57
There's a Story Behind Those Eyes	58
Reflection	59

PART 7: IT IS LIFE!

Delightful Confidence	63
Home Rejected Me	64
Forget Fear	65
Knock, Knock, Unlock!	66

Many Ventures	67
Steady Pace Friendship	68
Reflection	69
Acknowledgments	71
About Author	73

If you purchased this book without a cover, you should be aware that this book is stolen property. It was reported as "unsold and destroyed" to the publisher, and the author has not received payment for this "stripped book."

ISBN Number: 0-9960743-5-3 (Paperback)
ISBN Number: 0-9960743-4-6 (E-Book)
LCC Number: 2023906920

God Sent The Raven
Copyright © 2023 Raven Chasity Rogers
Edited by Cynthia M. Portalatín
Published by:

PO Box 1819, Owings Mills, MD 21117
www.maynetre.com

All rights reserved. Except for use in the case of brief quotations embodied in critical articles and reviews, the reproduction or utilization of this work in whole or part in any form by any electronic, digital, mechanical or other means, now known or hereafter invented, including xerography, photocopying, scanning, recording, or any information storage or retrieval system, is forbidden without written prior permission of the author and publisher.

The scanning, uploading, and distribution of this book via the Internet or via any other means without permission of the publisher and author is illegal and punishable by law. Purchase only authorized versions of this book, and do not participate in or encourage electronic piracy of copyrighted materials. Your support of the author's rights is appreciated.

This is a work of fiction. Names, characters, places, and incidents are products of the author's imagination, the author's own personal experience, or are used fictitiously and are not to be construed as real. While the author was inspired in part by actual events, the characters are not distantly inspired by any individual known or unknown to the author. Any resemblance to actual events, locales, business establishments, organizations, or persons, living or dead, is entirely coincidental.

Printed in the United States of America
First Printing 2023
10 9 8 7 6 5 4 3 2 1

Dedication

To the one and only, The Ultimate Homie (Holy Spirit), for always guiding me.
In Loving Memory
Sheree Renee Rogers
(My Beloved Mother)
&
Raun Rogers
(My Sweet Brother & "Irish Twin")

Foreword

TREMAYNE MOORE, AUTHOR & PUBLISHER

Every once in a while, I have met people who have touched my life. What brings me joy is meeting someone who shares a passion for writing and touching the world. As I was reading some of Raven's poems, I was taken aback (in a good way), and believe that her voice needs to be heard.

I believe that positive voices are so needed in this world today.

If you have never read poetry, you are going to be in for a treat. If you are an avid poetry lover, you are really going to be in for a treat. If you have an ear to hear and a heart to listen, get ready!! May Raven's writing touch your heart and soul.

Part 1: It Is God!

God Sent The Raven!!!

11/28/2022

Good day all, my name is Raven.
Born and raised in Jersey City.
Please don't feel sorry for me! Don't need none of your pity.
God sent the Raven
Marked by the Most High, since the beginning of time!
Some great days more than others, I put that on a dime!
Hated by some, but always loved by so many.
A family fortune! Can't complain!
I have plenty!
Misunderstood, while I walked out this walk.
The prime focus to many, but the least one to talk!
God sent the Raven to the Earth, to bring Glory to His name!
So, please get out of my way, if you're not doing the same!

Dear Blue Skies

11/22/2022

Your amazing setting is a love story to my eyes.
As I gaze upon your splendor,
Sometimes, it's hard to wonder why.
When I need a chance to catch my breath,
All I do is look up; now I feel refreshed.

Wow! Oh my!
Help me! I just continue to stare.
You're like a beautiful painting,
So bonafide, yet so rare!

Immaculate! Oh, so radiant,
You just dwell in the sky
Can't imagine how one can, after seeing your beauty,
Turn around and say good-bye!

Stargaze

11/29/2022

Every time, I ponder on your goodness,
I suddenly go into a trance.
The beauty of the Galaxy you created always invites me to take a second glance.
The hypnotic effects of your wonder,
No one can copy.
If created by anyone else,
Everything would be sloppy!
Only You can allow me to fix my eyes, upon your creation.
The stars sit high above, during the night,
Like a blanket hovering over the nation.
As they show off their sparkle, gleaming in the sky.
The beauty of them leaves me speechless, and always wondering,
Why?

The Author of My Soul

12/12/2022

Many, many years ago,
Lord, You wrote the storyline for my life.
The script written wasn't anything strange to you.
Because You drafted me to be blessed and determined to pass right through.
This life is not fiction!
It is surely a fact!
The way You modify me, when I fall.
Immediately, You bless me to bounce right back.
God, You possess the script to my soul!
Only the narration of Your words can instantly make me whole!
The pleasure of having You as the author, grants me a life worth living!
And the purpose to fulfill Your will is the ultimate gift You are giving!

The Essence of You
11/20/2022

The essence of You Lord ...
Takes my breath away
Enlightens me to say
Strengthens me from day-to-day
Is where I lay

The essence of You, Lord ...
Is what so many can't find
Gives me peace of mind
Displays a love so gentle and kind
Is there all the time

The essence of You, Lord ...
Grants me direction, wherever I go
Is who, and what I know
So magnificent, You always show
Plays a harmonious flow

The essence of You, Lord
Leaves me impressed

RAVEN CHASITY ROGERS

Is always the best
Is worth fulfilling this beautiful quest
Provides to my unique soul rest

That Sunday Flow

12/01/2022

Get up! Get ready!
And put on your Sunday garments!
Out the door is where I'm heading,
Sunday service is almost starting!
The start of prayer and morning worship,
Giving all Glory to His Mighty name!
Testimony service young and old,
How our lives will never, ever be the same!
God's powerful Gospel ever told by the preacher!
His Holy truth will remain!
To be His witness throughout the world
A testament to everyone regardless of how they came!

The Ultimate Homie
11/27/2022

I get to share You with the world.
No magnifying glass, full exposure!
There's no need for an acquaintance, the dopest Best Friend! Yes! I'm sure!
I pray and submit the most deepest of secrets, before walking out the front door.
You handle all of my business, and it builds trust, more and more!
I opened my heart to help enemies, who stared me down to the floor.
And like the Ultimate Homie, Your power allowed me to soar.
In clear visions and dreams, You reveal to me, who you are!
The Magnificent Holy Spirit!
The real star that You are!
Some may never understand Your presence and deny the power there of.
But just like Jesus, the Heavenly Son, You also came from above.
Hallelujah! All the glory!
The best of friendships, you see!
Thank You, Ultimate Homie for always guiding me!

Reflection

Who do you think each poem within the section "It Is God" is written to?

_____
_____
_____
_____
_____

What comes to mind as you read each poem in this section?

_____
_____
_____
_____

What's your favorite line(s) in each poem within this section?

_____
_____
_____
_____
_____

REFLECTION

If you had to add another stanza to each poem within this section, what would you write?

_____
_____
_____
_____
_____

Part 2: It Is Me!

A Mirror of Me

11/28/2022

Open your eyes! Look up! What do you see?
Is it a reflection of Jesus all over me?
A mirror image of His character, from His word, to speak life!
If you see Him, right through me, no need to think twice.
To walk, talk and follow after true righteousness!
That beautiful mirror of me, you can see at its best!

Glisten Me, Please!

1/14/2023

Vibrant, perky, and sparkling like glitter!
Truthful radiance without a doubt.
Releasing good vibes when I enter your world.
No pressure! Unclog your ears! Hear me out!
Moving forward towards greatness!
A Great light shines upon me!
You will know that it's Holy Ghost inspired. It's evident! Can't you see?
Enjoying and counting blessings abundantly!
It's cool! Yes! It is written!
No need for a copyright.
He gave me permission!
To give you these words and commit to His truth!
Make room for all of His love!
Feel free to open up, because He's real proof!

I'm a Better Woman! For a Better Man!

2/20/2023

The quality of my garment,
Will I begin to unfold.
We are the keys to God's destined plan.
Hand-in-hand, we'll take hold!
Stripped of the damages, once branded.
On my life, no more control!
A better woman, handpicked from the ashes of death's highest toll.
For a better man, who conquered life's giants!
Serenaded by your striking skills.
Awarded by Heaven's secret information.
Hidden from the enemy to kill.
Groomed to be together,
Higher heights are ahead.
So, at last, we're better for each other.
Now let us march in God's stead!

Thankfully Single
1/09/2023

Greetings and good day.
Allow me to make the notion to say!
The details of my heart, must be shared on today!
Quite divine and charming, if I may.
Showing gratitude for singles is at bay!
No shame; it's temporary! No need to go astray!
I'm thankful to the Highest! The absolute – yay!
Identify distractions! Yet keep on moving, and every obstacle you will slay!
And walk the path that is chosen, because you're sure to align with the right mate someday!

The Power of My Tears

11/24/2022

The power of my tears
So gentle flowing from my eyes
Developed from the pain of rejection and abandonment
Formed deeply inside
False accusations with no explanation
They continue to stream down my face
The extreme challenges that life had to offer
Left me feeling distant and too out of place
A waterfall of anger, I had to leave it ALL behind
But the power of my tears washed it away!
Bringing love, joy, and new life to mind!

You Can't Put Out My Fire

12/26/2022

No matter how hard one may try, you can't put out my fire!
The power of the Great one has ignited a spark on the inside of me
That burns gracefully to the point where you have to admire.
Let's be honest! I'm too hot to grab a hold of!
Don't get upset! Please cool off!
And if there's a problem, consult that with the Mighty One from above!

Reflection

Who do you think each poem within the section "It Is Me" is written to?
_____
_____
_____
_____

What comes to mind as you read each poem in this section?
_____
_____
_____
_____

What's your favorite line(s) in each poem within this section?
_____
_____
_____
_____

REFLECTION

If you had to add another stanza to each poem within this section, what would you write?

_____
_____
_____
_____
_____

Part 3: It Is Love!

2 Different Time Zones of Love
11/25/2022

Our love is eight hours apart
Which symbolize new beginning
Many miles across the globe
Near your heart, is where I'm leaning!
Countless conversations, we have, no matter the time,
Your words make it hard to focus
It's a fight getting you off my mind.

Concentrate! Concentrate!
So much greatness to birth!
Our love ever so priceless,
Not many know what it's worth!
As I watch your funny videos,
It draws me closer to you.
That moment I hear your pure voice,
Instantly, stuck to you, just like glue.

2 Different Time Zones of Love
A testimony of great things to come!
We are blessed and special to God!
Saved by His dear Son!

A Bittersweet Lullaby
11/27/2022

Cradle me to sleep with your love, as your words of affirmation, serenade my ears, like a bittersweet lullaby.
As I hear the beating of your heart, it gives off lovely music notes, with a pitch so high.
Sing to me with the sound of your breath!
Inhale and exhale, to the harmony of you rocking me back and forth in your arms.
The peaceful melody of your love, is an escape from all the chaos and harm.
Flawlessly written and to my surprise,
When I embrace the act of your goodness and bittersweet lullaby!

A Lovely Valentine

11/24/2022

Celebrations, red hearts,
Chocolate bars, where to start?
The second month of the year,
On the 14th day, Yay! It's here!
A lovely Valentine it will be!
Cheers to you and cheers to me!

Crimson Love
11/15/2022

Your love is red and sharp
I wear it like the latest fashion
Leaves me so mesmerized!
Sometimes, I don't know what happened

Like bright effects of a solar eclipse
Just can't stare with my eyes
The crimson color so deep
It's the sweetest surprise!

Overflows, like a manifold of blessings,
It makes me want to scream
Feels like an evangelical sensation
If you know what I mean.

My Perky Love!
11/27/2022

Wow! OH MY!
I just continue to stare
Your body is a work of art,
Beautifully painted! Perky and rare!
You're a masterpiece of God's wonderful creation
Firmly standing there!
So immaculate and greatly handled with care.
Briskly! Your love for me, vastly fills the air
My perky love, you've changed my life in a way,
That so many would say, "it's not fair!"

Rose Petals

11/28/2022

Silky! Soft and elegant!
With a touch of your grace.
The softness of your character, adds a special touch to my face.
Separated, but when joined together, depict a symbol of our love.
It's the combination of your greatness!
Designed from Heaven above.

Our Absolute Love

12/01/2022

Must I sum up the total value of our love?
Absolutely, Sure!
You add to my life in the most amazing ways.
Subtracting from the nonsense that's so impure!
Dividing and sharing equally, all that we possess.
Multiplying a love so powerful as each day we confess.
Making our love the key factor as we continue to grow,
more and more the love we have for one another will always flow!

The Compass to My Heart

11/27/2022

Longitude, Latitude!
Get ready to start!
Here are some directions you need to follow, from the compass to my heart.
Don't go North, nor go South, or go East, Please! Go West!
And continue to walk closer 'til you hear the heart beat from my chest.
Don't go to the right or near the bottom towards the ground.
Go around to my left side and all my love, you will have found.
Without hesitation, don't move fast, just go slow!
Allow the compass to lead, just trust! You will know!
When you finally arrive, take a deep breath it is through!
Because the compass of my heart, led me directly to you.

Reflection

Who do you think each poem within the section "It Is Love" is written to?
_____
_____
_____
_____
_____

What comes to mind as you read each poem in this section?
_____
_____
_____
_____
_____

What's your favorite line(s) in each poem within this section?
_____
_____
_____
_____
_____

REFLECTION

If you had to add another stanza to each poem within this section, what would you write?

_____
_____
_____
_____
_____

Part 4: It Is Great!

A Glimpse of Fresh Air

9/21/2019

It was like a sudden miracle
My life began to change
When I had to let you go
Everything felt so strange

Just like a glimpse of fresh air
I was able to breathe again

Trusting in God with all that I am
I wasn't afraid anymore
Being open to love again
My heart was able to soar

Just like a glimpse of fresh air
I was able to breathe again
To experience all that love has to offer
Over and over again.

That Great Commencement!

11/27/2022

Congratulations, Graduates!
The day has finally come
Where your hard work has paid a ton.
A ton of time, sacrifice and tears, because you didn't quit! You now stand here!
Standing tall, head held high!
Let the loud sound of Victory, reach the sky!
The sky above is where you'll soar.
For some, the first of generations, an absolute score!
A score for the ages, as you carry on with success.
Walk in the path, where the light shines and walk into your best!
So many have come from near and far, For higher education; you set the bar.
A bar so heavy, it takes a special grace to carry.
To carry the load with patience, was enough to tarry.
Your best is what's appreciated! No matter what they say!
Remember this moving forward, every start of the day is a new day!
A new day to conquer all that's set before you,
As you climb over rocky challenges, like the shining morning Sun.

Recite this over your spirit! Indeed, I have already Won!
Won the reward, because someone greater paved the way before me. And now that time has come!
To celebrate that Great Commencement!
Congratulations, Graduates, all the hard work is done!!!

The Runway of Victory!!!

2/21/2023

The straight path is visible! I'm ready!
Forward is the way! So, let's go!
To strut down the runway of victory.
Left foot, right foot, left!
Just like that! It is so!
Every excuse has fallen by the wayside
Yes indeed! I have grown!
You don't have to be a spectator!
Or be hating on the low.
There's enough room on this runway
Strut with me! It's all love!
Now strike a pose, for your victory!
Already granted and demonstrated
From the Powerful One, up above!
Sashay with pizzazz!
Stomping over every one of life's challenges
That stands in your way.
Use the runway of victory to lead to conquest
As you embrace and overcome, day by day!

Reflection

Who do you think each poem within the section "It Is Great" is written to?
_____
_____
_____
_____

What comes to mind as you read each poem in this section?
_____
_____
_____
_____

What's your favorite line (s) in each poem within this section?
_____
_____
_____
_____

REFLECTION

If you had to add another stanza to each poem within this section, what would you write?

_____
_____
_____
_____
_____

Part 5: It Is Family!

Four: Four: Four (444)

11/14/2022

On the 4th day, of the 4th month, your tall body was seen by number 4.
My whole world stood still, as I opened the door.
In shock and disbelief, you lied there so peaceful, so sweet!
You left me here all alone, not to suffer defeat.
You were a star to so many, my favorite number 5.
I cannot believe it! You're no longer alive!
You were so young and yet gone way too soon.
My dope Irish twin, who came from the same womb.
When they pronounced your time of death, my heart broke, I was sore.
I did not ever expect to hear the time: 4:44.

"Rest In Paradise!"
Raun Rogers
08-07-1980 – 04-04-2020
I will always be your Irish twin.

I Cried for You
7/11/2018

It was a sad day
When I found out
They took you away
I cried for you

I cried for you
When you had to go
I cried for you
Trust and believe

That real, real soon
I'll no longer have to cry
Because your freedom will come
And you'll be seen
Like the earth and sky

(I love you, nephew)
This poem is dedicated to you
I cried for you
Because you kept silent ...

My Daddy! My Heart!

11/22/2022

Pop, you've allowed me to represent your last name
However, not many days hence
It will be for a short time
Because love will recompence
An opportunity to announce to the world
That I came from the "real" Roy Rogers.

My daddy, my heart, yes, all too real
That's True!
If I don't say anything else, I will say
Thank you for being you.

So many chances to leave,
So many reasons why
I hope my life has brought you joy
And happy tears from your eyes

Not sure what I have done to deserve you
But God always knew
Now, that's why I was birthed from your seed
100% TRUE!!!

Sixteen Crystals

7/3/2018

Sixteen crystals, so rare, so true
Sixteen crystals, birthed by you.

[Miraculously formed out of love]

Sixteen crystals formed in unique shapes, colors, and sizes.
Sixteen crystals unleashing a variety of surprises.

Sixteen crystals that sparkle like the stars above.
A gift from God miraculously formed with love.

Even though you now dwell with God above,
You leave behind sixteen crystals,
So pleasant like a dove.

[Rest in Heaven Mommy]
With love, Sixteen Crystals

Reflection

Who do you think each poem within the section "It Is Family" is written to?

_____
_____
_____
_____

What comes to mind as you read each poem in this section?

_____
_____
_____
_____

What's your favorite line (s) in each poem within this section?

_____
_____
_____
_____

REFLECTION

If you had to add another stanza to each poem within this section, what would you write?

_____
_____
_____
_____
_____

Part 6: It Is Clear!

A Tailored Lie

12/12/2022

Truthfully, there were some fun times in the beginning.
You developed a well-cut storyline
Until the bad signs started to manifest, and you no longer looked fine.
The garment of dishonesty, you wore it well!
Like a tailored outfit, delivered from the hole of hell.
How dare you think that you would get by
When all you've done was sow lie after lie?
Unfortunately, for you, there was no love lost.
However, trust and believe, you will pay the cost!

Distant Waves

12/01/2022

Loud sounds once roaring!
Come to find out, all you do is talk!
A manipulator towards many,
Just like you, never walk the walk.
So shallow, like a small puddle of water,
Don't make your presence known!
But like the trickster of a man, you are,
A true clown is how you're shown!
Crashing and hitting rocks is what your life is like.
Don't you dare come any closer!
Because you're definitely not my type.
Therefore, please respect my boundaries
And give me all of my space!
Let's be clear, like the distant waves!
And stay far away from this place!

If I Have to Beg

12/26/2022

Back and forth
To and from
I give; you take
More and more
Wow! If I have to beg, this should be no more!
When it's meant to be,
It will flow freely through an open door!
Yet, willingly enter my life, like a radiant and majestic light never seen before!
So confident! No need to beg or plea!
It's a guarantee!
What God has for me will always be for me!

Invisible Butterfly
01/14/2023

Incognito, you are!
Always needy! Yet, nowhere to be found.
The road to selfishness, you drive with ease.
A comfortable habit that has you so far bound!
Unapologetically, ghosting is how you move!
Concealing its true identity! But who are you?
Like the butterfly inside the cocoon, you're getting ready to morph!
Unreliable and shameful, you hesitate to come forth.
Beautiful and colorful are the butterflies that I see.
When I need you to show up, you're never there for me.
I hold dear to the truth, and I give you a chance.
How invisible are you? I can't get a glance!
Some words of expression, as I put this to rest!
Stop living a lifestyle of secrecy! And let me see you at your best!

The Looking Glass
12/12/2022

Vivid images of him, You saw straight through.
Distinctively, clear and visible You've shown me what's true!
He tried to prey on me with his charm and lies.
And with insight from the looking glass, You revealed his deceit before my eyes.
The power of your discernment gave way to a beautiful light!
But having no ounce of regret, You allowed me to see early on that he wasn't right!

There's a Story Behind Those Eyes

11/14/2022

There's a story behind those eyes
If you begin to tell me,
I need to know,
Will I be surprised?

I'm curious to know
Is it a story of love?
Or a deep dark mystery
You wear like a glove?

Again, I'm curious to know
Where does it take place?
Does the plot have a twist?
There's no time to waste!

A climax so suspenseful
No joy and no laughter,
Should I wait till the end
For that happily ever after?

Reflection

Who do you think each poem within the section "It Is Clear" is written to?

_____
_____
_____
_____

What comes to mind as you read each poem in this section?

_____
_____
_____
_____

What's your favorite line(s) in each poem within this section?

_____
_____
_____
_____

REFLECTION

If you had to add another stanza to each poem within this section, what would you write?

_____
_____
_____
_____
_____

Part 7: It Is Life!

Delightful Confidence

12/26/2022

It's with great pleasure and extreme applause!
To see you hate my confidence in life, but what's your cause?
Very tasty and delightful to the fulfilling of my soul!
And entreat my confidence to be contagious to others, that's my new found goal!
When I seek after the Highest of High, His desires towards me show true!
No need to be bland or artificial!
My advice to you: open up to a confidence so delightful, knowing He can do the same for you!

Home Rejected Me

11/28/2022

Guess what?! Home rejected me, but that is okay!
It was never my place, from the very beginning to stay.
New horizons are waiting for me, to overcome, I say!
My destiny to fulfill! Forever, I may!
Home was just a place, where my head only would lay.
No need to settle, because there's a new home today.

Forget Fear
1/8/2023

Without a sense to recall,
Forget every emotion of doubt!
March on one step further!
You are sure to come out!
Be discreet! You can do it!
Just give it a try!
Forget, and tell fear: You're irrelevant!
You've been rejected! Now good-bye!
At this point in your life, trust God and stand tall!
Forget fear! Put it behind you!
Don't be afraid! You won't fall!
Take a moment and a deep breath!
Clear your mind and refresh!
Go after all that is yours!
After all, a new quest is approaching
With the master key to open doors.

Knock, Knock, Unlock!

2/20/2023

Knock, Knock!
Tick tock, tick tock!
Don't look at the clock!
Your insecurities are ready for you to unlock!

Drop off all your uncertainties,
And pick up your confidence
At the end of the block!
Rebirth the love you have travailing on the inside, because there's so much more in stock.

Embrace a new dawning!
Don't let go! Just hold tight!
And expose all that's within you!
No more insecurities! Just pure light!

Many Ventures
12/12/2022

Tiny! Microscopic! Large and gigantic!
Are you willing to come along for the ride?
Unpleasant process after process.
Just stay the entire course!
There's a great promise inside.
Glorious hopes and dreams, you once had buried.
Now, is the time to dig them up.
Be jolly! Yet, hurry!
What a daring experience as you drive down memory lane.
Through mountains and valleys, nothing is ever quite the same.
Take a risk! Live your life! And you will begin to see what's new!
There are many ventures about living, and they will, no doubt, show you the real you!

Steady Pace Friendship
01/14/2023

Hey, you! Patience! Patience!
Why must you rush?
We just met a short time ago.
What's all the fuss?
Our friendship is just beginning.
One step for you, and one step for me.
Let's see what can blossom!
When we allow our steady friendship to be.

Reflection

Who do you think each poem within the section "It Is Life" is written to?
_____
_____
_____
_____
_____

What comes to mind as you read each poem in this section?
_____
_____
_____
_____
_____

What's your favorite line(s) in each poem within this section?
_____
_____
_____
_____
_____

REFLECTION

If you had to add another stanza to each poem within this section, what would you write?

_____
_____
_____
_____
_____

Acknowledgments

A special shout out and extreme thank you, to my Lord and Savior, Jesus Christ, who allowed me to pen these beautiful poems at the right time. He blessed me with this amazing gift, to use the power of my words, in the poetic form. Without Him, this book would not be possible.

A Special Thanks

Special thanks to my father, the genuine, Mr. Roy Rogers, who sacrificed so much for my family and I. To my only oldest brother Roy Ross and my dope little brothers Reinod Rogers and Ren Rogers. I appreciate all of the love and support, that the three of you have shown me. To my entire family, I love y'all and thank you. To Pastor Tremayne Moore, my mentor/publisher, for encouraging and pushing me to write this great book. To my wonderful "Angel" on planet Earth, Mother JoAnne Grant! You truly have been amazing and a blessing to my life. To my "Jersey Mentor," Elder Jeffrey Chazz Williams, for blessing me with words of encouragement and wisdom in the things of God. I can't forget the homie Michael D. Davis, who has been an absolute blessing to me in good and bad times.

About Author

Raven Chasity Rogers is the 4th of 16 children, who also served in the United States Navy. She holds an Associate of Arts Degree in Early Childhood Education from Hudson County Community College, a Bachelor of Arts Degree in English (Cum Laude) from Kean University, and completed the Child Advocacy and Policy Certificate Program from Montclair State University in New Jersey. Raven enjoys writing poetry while embracing her best life, and her foundational scripture is based on Lamentations 3:22-24.

www.ingramcontent.com/pod-product-compliance
Lightning Source LLC
Chambersburg PA
CBHW071627040426
42452CB00009B/1516